This
Whitaker Playhouse
Book Belongs To:

In Him was life; and the life was the light of men.

John 1:4

All Scripture quotations are taken from the King James Version Easy Read Bible, KJVER®, © 2001, 2007, 2010, 2015 by Whitaker House. Used by permission. All rights reserved.

THE STORY OF RUTH
www.philsmouse.com
ISBN: 978-1-64123-610-2
© 2021 by Phil A. Smouse

Whitaker House
1030 Hunt Valley Circle
New Kensington, PA 15068
www.whitakerhouse.com

All rights reserved. No part of this publication may be reproduced or transmitted for commercial purposes, except for brief quotations in printed reviews, without written permission of the publisher. Churches and other non-commercial interests may reproduce portions of this book without the express written permission of Whitaker Corporation, provided that the text does not exceed 500 words or 5 percent of the entire book, whichever is less, and that the text is not material quoted from another publisher. When reproducing text from this book, include the following credit line: "THE STORY OF RUTH, published by Whitaker Corporation. Used by permission."

A Note to Parents...
Your word is a lamp to my feet, and a light to my path. Psalm 119:105

if you love the wonderful, rollicking rhythm and rhyme of the classic picture books you read as a child and want to bring that same sense of joy to your children, you're in the right place.

Learning, understanding, and living God's Word is a journey that lasts a lifetime. And that journey starts by reading God's Word. Every tiny heart on the face of this earth is trying to find its way home to Jesus. And God's eternal promise to our precious little lambs is that they will find Him—when we take the time to show them how and where to look.

Jesus wants us to be His—one hundred percent. And the most important thing is not what we say or do, or even who we reach. The most important thing is the relationship we cultivate with Him.

That deep spiritual connection isn't only for adults. The truths you share with your children from God's Word will stay with them for the rest of their lives. This delightful, child-friendly Bible story is a perfect way to introduce those precious little ones to the joy of a heart filled with Jesus and the knowledge of God's Word.

Phil A. Smouse

Where you go, I will go.
Ruth 1:16

it can't be true....

I can't go on!
Oh, everything we had is gone."
Naomi wept. Poor Ruthie cried.
Naomi's precious sons had died!

And oh, one precious,
priceless son,
Naomi's son,
that very one,
*was Ruthie's
husband.*

Lord above!
Her one-and-only,
one true love.

Now, sometimes when it rains it pours,
and this time it would pour for sure.

For evil people ruled the land
as evil people sometimes can
and sometimes will and sometimes do,
when you and I allow them to.

From here to there, from there to here,
the food began to disappear!
It filled the people full of fear—
yes, full of fear from ear to ear!

"Orpah! Ruth!" Naomi cried.
"The time has come. We must decide.
We have to leave. We cannot stay.
We cannot stay, not now—no way.

From north to south, from west to east,
the men are gone. Extinct. Deceased!
Without a man," Naomi said,
"WE'RE ALL ABOUT AS GOOD AS DEAD!"

(Now ladies, things were different then,
so don't get too upset, amen?)

"Just look at me. I'm old and wrinkled,
sagged and bagged and crook'd and
crinkled — crumpled, puckered,
nooked and crannied, Rip-Van-
Winkled, grayed and grannied!

*Oh, there's just no hope in sight
to find another Mister-Right,
or even just a Daffy Duck,
an Elmer Fudd, or Mister Yuck!*

The time has come! The time is now.
The time has come right now and how!
You must return, you must, I say,
return back home, right now, today."

Naomi prayed
they'd see the light
and Orpah knew
that she was right.

She packed her bags
without a fight
and left for home
that very night.

But oh, not Ruth.
Not her. No way.
She had a thing
or two to say. . .

"I can't return. I want to stay.
I will NOT go, right now, today!"

"For where you are
is where I'll be.
And when you stay,
you'll stay with me.

And when you die,
I'll die with you.
And THAT is what
I'm going to do.

*Your God will be MY God, and He
will surely care for you and me!"*

Oh, what a thing for Ruth to say.
That kind of thing can make your day,
and make you shout
"hip-hip hooray!"

They hugged and kissed,
 then packed up tight
and left for Bethlehem
that night.

"Naomi! Is it really true?
What happened, girl? Just look at you!

Your hair! Your clothes! Your shoes! Your toes!
Your eyes, your ears, your mouth, your nose!
You're looking pale. You're looking thin.
In fact, if we may say again,
you're really looking more akin
to something that the cat dragged in!"

Well, things looked bad, the way things can,
but listen now, God had a plan. . .

"Oh Naomi, please don't cry.
Oh please don't cry. I'll tell you why.

I'll find a farm. I'll be real nice.
I'll ask them once or maybe twice
to take our jugs and jars and sacks
and fill them full of treats and snacks."

"Yes, crumbs and morsels, flakes and flecks, leftover kernels, crumbs and specks. A black banana! Bagels! Lox! Some cheese stuck to a pizza-box!
 I'll beg and plead. I'll sob and bleat! I'll ask them for a tasty treat—
An itsy-bitsy, teeny-weeny, tiny scrap for us to eat!"

So off she went. She did her thing. She did it never noticing that someone had been fastening his bulging eyes on *everything*.

"Who IS that girl out in my field
and what's she doing?" Boaz squealed.
"Look AT that hair. Look AT those eyes!
Excuse me just one minute, guys,
I've got to go and *socialize!*"

He shaved his toes. He licked his lips.
He checked his teeth for cracks and chips.
He combed the bugs out of his hair,
yes, Don Juan double-debonair
with savoir-faire extraordinaire!

Now don't be quick to judge, amen?
Well, don't think what you're thinking then.
For Boaz was a gentleman.

"Please stay with us. Take what you need.
Take what you need and more, indeed!"

He loaded up all Ruthie's sacks
and jugs and jars with treats and snacks.
Yes, it WAS *true-love* at first sight—
a double thumping-heart delight!

She headed home. *Oh, what she'd found!*
Her world was turning upside-down.
She ran the whole way back to town
about ten feet above the ground.

"I'm telling you, tonight's the night,"
Naomi grinned, "and if I'm right,
there's only one thing left to do
to get that man to say I DO!"

So do they did. Oh, DID they do...

They fluffed and puffed. They crimped and curled.
They powdered, sweet-perfumed, and pearled!
They thanked the Lord. They sang His praise!
They marveled at His wondrous ways!

And off she went into the night
to have and hold her Mister Right—
her Mister Shining-Armored Knight—
her straight-from-heaven-sent delight!

Now, as I'm sure that you supposed, *Boaz said "YES!"* when Ruth proposed.
They tied the knot and lived to be quite happy ever-afterly.
And soon God blessed them with a son, a precious, little baby one.

Take a second. Think it through. Oh, what God will go and do!
For God is love and love is kind, the kindest that you'll ever find,
the kindest that you'll ever see.

That's something else—don't you agree?

All that you say to me I will do.
Ruth 3:5

There's still more fun from Whitaker Playhouse.

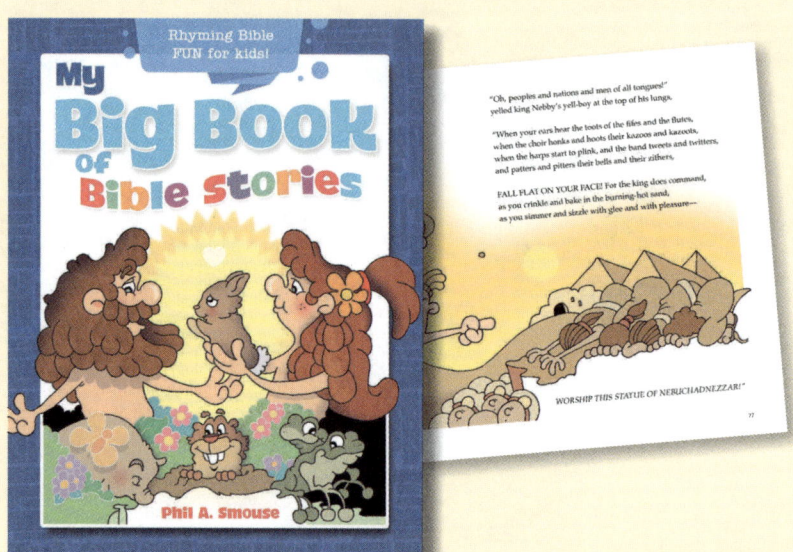

My Big Book of Bible Stories
978-1-64123-548-8

From award-winning author and illustrator Phil A. Smouse, *My Big Book of Bible Stories* features seventeen favorite Bible stories told in hilarious rhymes, with bright, full-color illustrations. These clever retellings of key Scriptures from the Old and New Testaments include the stories of creation, Adam and Eve, Jonah, the Good Samaritan, Jesus and Nicodemus, Peter, and more. Parents will enjoy reading *My Big Book of Bible Stories* to their preschool children, while young readers will delight in the whimsical story-telling and artwork.

My Big Book of Bible People, Places, and Things
978-1-64123-549-5

This brand-new Bible dictionary for kids features 750 entries with witty, age-appropriate text and colorful illustrations from award-winning author and illustrator Phil A. Smouse. *My Big Book of Bible People, Places, and Things* explains important terms in simple ways that young readers can easily grasp, while the full-color illustrations enhance your child's learning. With such entries as "Alleluia," "Book of Life," "Mary and Martha," and "Walking on Water," this book provides an important head start to scriptural literacy.

whitakerplayhouse.com

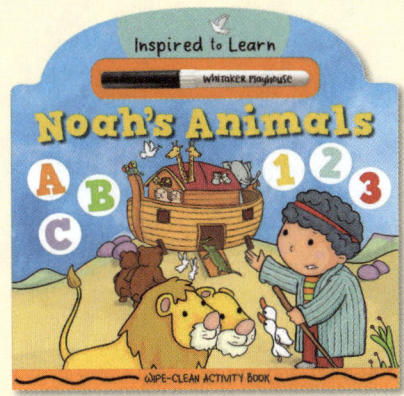
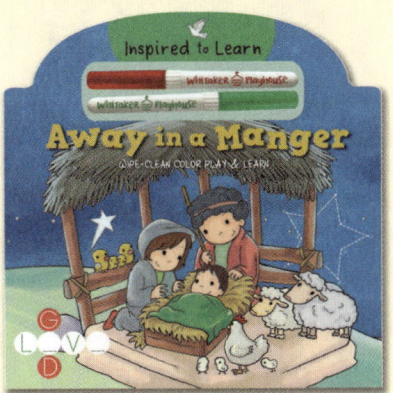

Bible ABCs   978-1-64123-428-3

Noah's Animals   978-1-64123-429-0

Away in a Manger   978-1-64123-527-3

Bible Activities   978-1-64123-430-6

Bible 123s   978-1-64123-427-6

Merry Christmas   978-1-64123-528-0

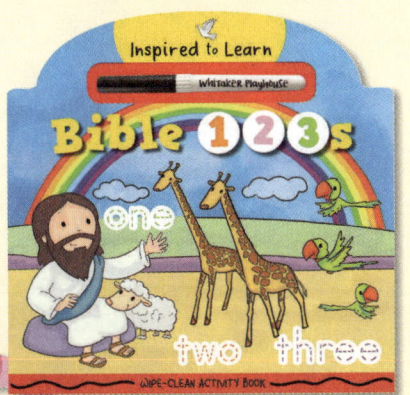

Wipe-Clean Activity Books

The *Inspired to Learn* series from Whitaker Playhouse is a perfect way for parents to share God's love with children while also introducing early learning concepts in a fun, interactive way.

These durable, wipe-clean books will provide hours of entertainment as children learn counting, the alphabet, color and shape recognition, drawing, spotting differences, and more. Parents will delight in their little one's progress as they enjoy the creative exercises.